SAILBOAT RACING

CLAIRE JONES

Lerner Publications Company • Minneapolis, Minnesota

ACKNOWLEDGEMENTS: The photographs are reproduced through the courtesy of: pp. 2, 5, 13, 20, 35, Tanzer Industries Ltd.; p. 4, The Science Museum, London; pp. 6, 21, 22, 24, Claire Jones; pp. 7, 14, 17, 19, 28, 30, *Sea Spray;* pp. 10, 25, 27, Surfglas, Inc.; p. 11, Performance Sailcraft International Company Ltd.; p. 15, John Mallitte; pp. 16, 42, Tom Vandervoort; p. 31 (left and right), Alan Warwick Yacht Designs; p. 32, Hutchwilco Life Jackets; p. 36, United States Naval Institute; p. 39, Whitbread & Company Ltd.; p. 40, Operation Sail 1976; p. 41, Ian Keith; p. 47, Jana Soeldner Danger. Cover photograph: Tanzer Industries Ltd. The publisher also wishes to acknowledge the editorial assistance of Jana Soeldner Danger, Edward M. Larson, and Tom Vandervoort.
The words "America's Cup" are registered trademarks of the New York Yacht Club.

LIBRARY OF CONGRESS CATALOGING IN PUBLICATION DATA

Jones, Claire.
    Sailboat racing.

    (Superwheels and thrill sports)
    SUMMARY: An introduction to the sport of sailboat racing, including its history, the fundamentals of sailing, the parts of a sailboat, safety rules, and racing classes.

    1. Sailboat racing—Juvenile literature. [1. Sailboat racing] I. Title. II. Series.

GV826.5.J63   797.1/4   80-12846
ISBN 0-8225-0434-0   (lib. bdg.)

Manufactured in the United States of America. Published simultaneously in Canada by J. M. Dent & Sons (Canada) Ltd., Don Mills, Ontario.

International Standard Book Number: 0-8225-0434-0
Library of Congress Catalog Card Number: 80-12846

1 2 3 4 5 6 7 8 9 10 87 86 85 84 83 82 81

YESTERDAY AND TODAY

Today thousands of people all over the world race sailboats as a sport. These people spend much of their spare time keeping their boats in winning condition for the next race. For many years, however, only the very rich could afford to sail for pleasure.

The first recorded sailboat race that was for sport—and for a bet—took place in England on October 1, 1661. King Charles II's crew raced the 49-foot (14.7-meter) yacht *Katherine* against the Duke of York's 51-foot (15.3-meter) vessel *Anne* for a stake of 100 pounds. Of course when people heard that the king enjoyed sailboat racing, they became interested in it, too. Sailboat racing quickly inspired a passion that spread throughout the British aristocracy. One man actually had his racing yacht built in the style of a fighting ship, complete with gun ports.

While the rich were developing sailboat racing as a sport, captains of cargo ships were racing for profit. During the 1800s, sailing ships, including America's great clipper ships, served as an important means of transporting goods and passengers. The captains of these ships raced because the first to arrive at his destination sold more goods and so made more money. Many captains also loved the challenge and excitement of racing. When two sailing ships bound for the same destination left a port together, the captains drove their vessels as hard as they dared. Each was determined to prove his ship superior.

Meanwhile, the sport of sailboat racing was spreading. In the early 1800s, it came to the United States. However, rich people still owned most of the *yachts*—boats used for racing or pleasure—and hired crews to race them.

3

The *Taeping* and the *Ariel* were two American clipper ships that sailed the seas during the 1800s.

In 1844, a group of yacht owners created the New York Yacht Club. A year later, the club held its first *regatta,* an event that includes a series of races and festivities held on one day or within a few days of each other. For that first event in 1845, club members raced nine boats. The New York Yacht Club has held regattas every year since.

As yacht racing became more popular, boat designs changed a great deal. Designers began to create more moderate-sized boats, and sailors in various parts of the United States raced them. Today sailboats come in all shapes and sizes, from tiny day sailers to large, ocean-going yachts. People from all income levels and with different degrees of skill participate in this thrilling water sport. Some owners may prefer to simply cruise their sleek and beautiful sailboats in lovely surroundings—on lakes, rivers, inlets, and oceans. These boats respond like living animals to the movements of wind and water. No wonder so many people are intrigued with the art of mastering sailboats and racing them to victory.

A modern racing sailboat

These small sailboats are being prepared for a race.

THE ART OF SAILING

The simplest sailboat consists of a floating *hull,* or body, supporting a *mast,* or vertical pole with a triangular piece of cloth *(sail)* attached to the mast. By fastening rope to the outer corner of the sail, a sailor can control its position and catch the wind. As the wind hits the sail, the boat moves forward. To move in a direction other than that of the wind, a sailor must use a rudder and tiller to steer the boat.

A simple boat may not go very fast, but several things can be done to improve its speed. Lightening the hull allows the boat to skim across the water faster. Streamlining the hull reduces the amount of hull in contact with the water, so there is less *drag* (resistance). Using a larger sail to catch more wind or adding a second sail also increases the boat's speed.

The boat in the foreground is using a second sail called a spinnaker to increase its speed.

PARTS OF A SAILBOAT

boom—A pole fastened horizontally to the mast to which the lower edge of the mainsail is attached

bow—The front end of a boat

centerboard—A board that can be raised and lowered through a slot in the bottom of a boat

hull—The body of a boat, not including masts, rigging, sails, and other gear

jib—A small triangular sail set on the front of a boat

mainsail—A boat's principal sail

main sheet—A line used to adjust the position of the mainsail

mast—A vertical pole fitted through or to the top of the deck. Sails are attached to the mast so that they can be hoisted to catch the wind.

rudder—A flat piece of metal or wood that extends into the water near the stern and is used to steer the boat

stern—The back end of a boat

tiller—A long handle that is used to turn the rudder

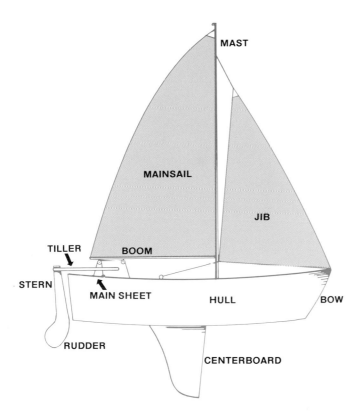

MAST

MAINSAIL

JIB

TILLER

BOOM

STERN

MAIN SHEET

HULL

BOW

RUDDER

CENTERBOARD

These improvements may make the boat move more quickly, but they also make it less stable. It would be useless to have a hull that slipped swiftly through the water if a boat always leaned to one side because of a lack of weight. An extreme *heel,* or tilt, spills wind from the sails and puts a different part of the hull under water. This tilt could easily spoil a boat's racing performance.

Measures that increase a boat's speed but make it less stable often cause the boat to *capsize,* or tip over. A small sailboat like a centerboard dinghy usually tips over fairly easily. To prevent this, a skipper and crew may put all their weight on the side opposite the heel or even hang over the edge to keep the boat sailing forward. Reducing a boat's heel in this manner is called *hiking out.*

The crew members of this catamaran, or double-hulled sailboat, are hiking to keep the boat from capsizing.

Hiking out in a Laser one-person dinghy

Most larger boats do not have such a problem with stability. They usually have lead or cast-iron keels that provide enough weight below the waterline. Even if a large boat with a deep keel is knocked flat to one side by the wind, it is designed to right itself immediately.

Today, with the help of computers, sailboats are being designed so they are both fast and safe. Various modern materials are used to make boats much lighter than those early sailing vessels. Sails and *line* (rope) are usually made of Dacron; cleats and blocks of plastic; masts and booms of aluminum; and hulls of fiberglass or plywood. These materials weigh less but give the boat extra strength. The weight of a boat is important because in moderate and light winds a lighter boat usually moves faster than a heavier one of similar design.

Yet a well-designed sailboat can't win a race without a good sailor. A sailor must be able to move the boat well, no matter what the direction or the strength of the wind. A sailboat can move three directions in relation to the wind: toward the wind, across the wind, and with the wind. A sailor must know how to best sail these *points of sail,* or directions, in order to win races.

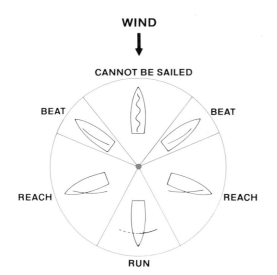

The basic sailing positions and how they relate to the direction of the wind

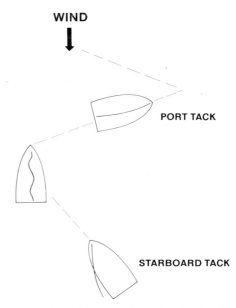

Beating to windward in a series of tacks (sailing into the wind)

A boat sailing toward the wind is *beating to windward,* or *on a beat.* If a sailboat attempts to sail directly into the wind the sail *luffs,* or flaps wildly, so a skipper must *tack,* or take a zigzag course. On this point of sail, the skipper pulls the sail in close to the center of the boat and the hull will heel sharply.

Two Tanzer racers beating to windward

Cherub-class dinghies on a reach

A boat sailing across the wind is said to be *reaching,* or *on a reach.* The boat's sails make about a 45-degree angle with the hull, forming powerful, rounded curves. Some light sailboats with flat bottoms can move fast enough when reaching to lift out of the water and *plane* across its surface.

A boat sailing with the wind is *running,* or *on a run.* At this point of sail, the wind comes across the stern of the boat, and the sails form an almost flat surface perpendicular to the hull.

Most sailboat races begin with everyone beating to windward to the first *windward mark,* or turning point. Courses usually include a reach and a run as well, so that skippers must compete on all points of sail.

Ocean racers running

CLASS RACING

Boats that are similar in size, shape, weight, and other specifications may be grouped together in a class. For example, more than a million centerboard sailing dinghies race in the world, and most of them belong to one of 950 different classes. Boats of the same class usually sail at about the same speed, so their skippers have equal chances in a race. The skill of the sailors, not the speed of the boats, determines the winner.

Most sailing clubs hold races for just a few classes. One club might, for example, schedule separate races for *Optimists, OK dinghies,* and *International 14s.*

The 8-foot Optimist, a type of centerboard dinghy, is the smallest boat in class racing. Optimists must meet strict specifications for hull size, shape, and materials, as well as weight, buoyancy, and mast and sail plans.

An eight-foot dinghy

Since almost all Optimists are identical, they are called a *one-design class*. Optimists are especially designed so that young people can sail them. In fact, no one over 15 may take part in the official races. Young sailors from all over the United States compete in the national championship races for Optimists. Because the International Yacht Racing Union (IYRU) recognizes the Optimist design as international, there are also international championships for these small boats.

In contrast, the IYRU does not recognize the OK dinghy, another one-design boat, as an international class. Nevertheless, owners of the nearly 14,000 OK dinghies still hold world championship races. A class association that has strong support from its members holds gatherings so people from different clubs can race.

Sailboats competing in the OK dinghy class

International 14s belong to a *restricted* or *development class* rather than a one-design class. Boats in a restricted class must be alike in certain ways but may differ in others. All International 14s must be similar in length, *beam* (width), and weight. But class rules place no limits on design, so sailors can keep pace with new developments. For that reason, International 14s have remained popular since 1923.

A few sailboat classes are unrestricted and give sailors quite a bit of freedom. For example, skippers may choose different *rigs* (arrangements of masts and sails) to fit the wind on the day of the race. Some class rules even permit sailors to use any beam, shape, and weight. This kind of freedom often leads to spectacular racing.

The different classes of sailboats offer different racing experiences. Shape, size, sail area, cost, and the skill required of the skipper vary tremendously from boat to boat. When choosing a craft, a person should know where the boat will be used—on a lake or river, in an inlet of the sea, or offshore—and should also find out which classes are raced in the area. A person who buys a boat for which no local clubs hold races may have no one to compete with.

Sometimes a type of boat may become popular even though it is not recognized officially by anyone except members of its own association. From such a beginning, a class may develop and eventually achieve national or international status. The United States Yacht Racing Union (USYRU), a member of the IYRU, has committees that determine which classes of boats receive national status. These committees also recommend to the IYRU which classes should be given international status.

The USYRU also recommends sailboat classes for the Olympic Games. Six different classes race in the Olympics, and they may change each time the games are held.

These sailboats belong to the 470 or light two-person dinghy Olympic class.

HANDICAP AND LEVEL-RATED RACING

Sailboats of different sizes and speeds often race together. People have developed ways of measuring differences between boats so that the skippers have equal chances to win. Once experts have determined how fast a boat should go under ideal conditions, they give it a rating. The rating compares that boat's speed with the speeds of other sailboats.

When a new yacht is built, or an old one changed, the owner must get a rating in order to enter many races. An official measures the boat's hull, spars, and sails. The official also records other technical information about the boat. A computer then analyzes the data and comes up with a printout, which becomes the yacht's rating certificate. This certificate permits the skipper to enter the yacht in handicap races.

In a handicap race, this small Tanzer 22 racer could win over large ocean racers like those pictured on the opposite page.

Race officials use ratings to determine handicaps for boats competing in a handicap race. A faster boat is given a *handicap*, or disadvantage when competing against a slower boat. Usually handicaps are measured in terms of *time allowances*. A time allowance tells how many seconds a boat travels for

each mile of the race. A bigger, faster boat must "give extra time" to a smaller, slower boat with a lower rating. This means that the faster boat must cross the finish line a certain amount of time ahead of its slower competitor in order to win. Because crossing the line first doesn't always guarantee a victory, many sailors lose some of the thrill of racing the last leg of the race.

To increase the excitement of competing, sailors have developed *level-rated classes*. In these classes, boats may look very different, but all have the same rating. Short, fat boats and long, skinny ones may race against each other. The designer of each boat has traded off one thing for another. Some may have deep keels, and others may have centerboards. But in spite of the differences, the boats rate the same and can race together on an equal basis. When boats in a race all have the same rating, no time allowance is needed and the first one to finish wins. But if level raters want to race against boats with ratings different than theirs, then they are given a time allowance.

The crew of a sailboat prepares for a big race.

THE DAY OF THE RACE

In a race, tension and excitement run high no matter what kind of boats are competing. Racing with a centerboard dinghy can be as much fun as competing with a huge ocean-going yacht. Skipper and crew must use all their skills to meet the challenge of their competitors.

On the day of the race, sailors listen to the weather forecast before they leave home, or they read the details on their club bulletin boards. If the race is for light boats and strong winds are forecast, skippers may take heavier or extra crew members. Added weight makes boats more stable in high winds.

The first thing the crew does when it climbs aboard is to adjust the sails and masts to make the most of the expected wind. Meanwhile, the skipper receives the details of the course. On the race committee boat, the sailing club's officers are making their own preparations for the race.

Ten minutes before the start of the race, the race officers hoist a white flag. They bring it down four-and-a-half minutes later. A second flag, a blue one, goes up after 30 seconds. This flag then goes down 30 seconds before the race starts. Skippers and crews use stopwatches to count down the final seconds while maneuvering for the best possible starting position. They try to arrive at the starting line at the exact moment an official fires the starting gun. Because the gun may fail to go off, officials also raise a third flag (red) or a larger visual signal at the start of the race.

Race officials make sure no boat crosses the starting line before the gun. They call back the skipper of any boat that goes over the line ahead of time, and the offender must return and cross the line again. But doing so may not be easy because this skipper must give *right-of-way* or allow the skippers

In this picture, the boat on the left is on a port tack and must give way to the other three boats, which are on starboard tacks.

who started correctly to go ahead. With boats crisscrossing in all directions due to early starters, the beginning of a race may be quite confusing.

There are many rules and regulations to master in sailboat racing. The most important rule states that boats on a *starboard tack* have right-of-way over boats on a *port tack*. A boat is on a starboard tack when the wind is coming over the starboard, or right side. This rule applies even when boats are not racing.

After starting, racers head for the first *mark*. A mark is an object used to indicate part of a race course. The first mark is usually

Prindle 16 catamarans beating to the first mark in a race

either a brightly colored buoy or flag that race officials have anchored in place, or a permanent feature of the landscape, such as a rock or an island. The course instructions state whether boats should leave each mark to port or starboard.

Since the first leg of the race is usually into the wind, skippers often *tack*, or sail a zigzag course, to the first mark. A skipper who approaches the mark on a starboard tack will probably have an advantage, but other rules also govern right-of-way at marks. The sailor who knows the rules can move ahead with confidence, while those who are unsure hang back rather than risk disqualification.

By the time the sailors approach the first mark, they usually have a feel for the way their boats are responding to the wind and waves. The boats may begin to spread out, giving skippers a chance to judge their competition and to decide how to get ahead.

Good sailors win through a combination of tactics. In addition to knowing the rules, skippers and crew members must be able to handle their boats skillfully. Every sailboat race is a series of encounters in which sailors steal past the boats ahead or fight off the ones behind. Crew members struggle to keep their spinnaker filled so that their boat will move ahead quickly. Each skipper hopes to catch and use a puff of wind that a competitor misses. It can be especially helpful to catch a boat on the wrong tack so that the skipper of that boat must give right-of-way.

Knowing local waters helps, too. Skippers may be able to steal several yards by finding a back *eddy* (a current running contrary to the main current) where the tide creeps along the shore. Or they may discover a *channel* (a narrow, deep section of water between two shallow areas) deep enough to squeeze through at certain stages of the tide.

A fleet of catamarans tacking to windward

Cherub dinghies during a race

A good sailor must also know how the formation of the land affects wind direction and strength. A skipper and crew can learn these things by sailing the same stretch of water often. They may find that the wind picks up a little as they near an island or a point jutting out into the water, while in another place there may be dead calm.

Toward the end of the race, sailors actively compete with the few boats near them. Whether a boat is sailing with the potential winners or with the slower ones, the skipper and crew race hard. The sound of a gun means the first boat has crossed the finish line. Race officials usually fire a gun as the second and third boats cross the finish line, too.

Some sailors may disagree with the outcome of the race. If one skipper thinks another breaks a rule, the first one puts out a red protest flag when the incident occurs. When the race is over, the skipper who flagged the incident makes a formal protest to the race committee.

A committee of disinterested club members is selected to listen to both sides of the argument and to examine any other evidence. This protest committee decides whether anyone actually broke a rule. If someone did, the offender receives a penalty and is placed lower in the standings for the race.

Clubs award points for each race throughout the season. The skipper with the most points at the end of the season is the champion. Most clubs give trophies to the skippers with the highest scores. A winner usually keeps a trophy until the club declares a new champion. Winners of special events, open championships, and national and international races often receive trophies based on their performances during single races or a series of races.

The IYRU has standardized racing rules throughout the world so that there is no confusion when sailors move to another area or country. In the United States, the USYRU administers these international rules.

An OK dinghy rounds the first mark in a race.

SAFETY

Part of the tension and excitement of a sailboat race comes from the challenge of testing one's skill against the elements. Wind and waves can sometimes drive any sailboat to its limits and threaten to overpower it, whether it is a tiny Optimist or a huge ocean racer.

A centerboard dinghy overpowered by the wind capsizes. The mast and sails may lie flat on the water, or the boat may turn completely over so that the mast points straight down. A centerboard dinghy usually carries enough buoyant material in its hull so that it does not sink. Skipper and crew must, however, work hard to right the boat, bail out the water, *trim the sails* (spread them to catch the wind), and continue the race. Occasionally, in heavy wind, a boat may capsize so often during a race that the skipper finally gives up.

Righting a capsized dinghy

Crew members prefer to right capsized small boats quickly without taking the sails off the mast. First, the crew climbs onto the centerboard, which extends through the bottom of the boat. Next, the members pull on the sides of the boat or on some lines attached to the inside of the hull. This creates enough leverage to turn the boat upright again. When the boat is right, everyone starts to bail out the water. A boat full of water tips easily and is likely to capsize again. If the sails are still set, the wind may blow the boat over before the crew can get rid of the water. Sometimes it is necessary to swim around to the mast and take down the sails before the crew can manage the job of bailing.

The crew and skipper of this sailboat are wearing wet suits and life jackets to protect themselves in case of capsizing.

In warm water and pleasant weather, capsizing usually presents little danger. But when the water is cold, racers may quickly begin to suffer from exposure unless they are properly dressed. Many sailors wear divers' wet suits while racing dinghies to protect themselves if they fall into the water and to keep themselves warm while moving through the wind and spray. Others wear waterproof foul-weather gear and life jackets.

Most clubs send a rescue boat to accompany sailors during a race. The rescue boat keeps out of everyone's way but watches for those who may need help righting their boats or getting back to the dock.

One way to keep a boat from capsizing is to reduce the sail area. The sail can usually be made smaller by *reefing*, or pulling the bottom portion of the sail down the mast and tying it to the boom with short pieces of rope known as *reef points*. A reefed sail still functions effectively, but it catches less wind because its area is much smaller.

Another way to keep a boat from capsizing is to release the *mainsheet*, the rope that controls the position of the mainsail. When the skipper releases the sheet, the sail flaps free and the wind spills out of it, easing the pressure on the boat.

Playing the mainsheet is a good way to control a boat in a gusty wind. When a gust hits the sail, a skipper can release the sheet and loosen or ease the sail. Once the gust has passed, the skipper can pull the sheet and tighten the sail so it catches as much wind as possible. This technique allows the skipper to keep the full area of the mainsail flying. The boat will continue to move quickly during periods when the wind is less heavy, but it will not be overpowered during a gust.

Crew members who reef the sail lose the advantage of having the entire mainsail up at times when there is less wind.

A boat that is sailing in a heavy wind may take in a great deal of water over the side. A skipper may even be forced to sail single-handedly while the crew bails furiously, using anything from a cup to a bucket. Whatever the crew uses, however, must be secured to the boat so that the container is not lost in a capsize.

Yachts that race long distances offshore in events sanctioned by the IYRU must have several sefety provisions, including the ability to right themselves. Boats that compete in long races also must have enough bunks for half the crew so that everyone gets sufficient rest. In addition, these boats must have *heads*, or toilets, well-equipped *galleys*, or kitchens, fire-fighting equipment, bilge pumps, and sturdy guard rails. Life jackets, safety harnesses, life rings, life rafts, first-aid kits, and many other items help to prepare crew members for any serious emergency.

Once out of sight of land and lighthouses, a sailor may find it difficult to keep a boat on course. For that reason, every boat should have a skilled navigator and good navigational equipment aboard. A navigator must be able to keep on course by using a radio direction finder, a compass, or a *sextant*. Navigators use sextants for *celestial navigation*, which depends on the sun, moon, stars, and planets for keeping the boat on course.

35

A painting of the schooner *America* by C. G. Evers. When this famous boat won the English Yacht Races in 1851, the America's Cup competition got its start.

GREAT RACES

The general public usually doesn't pay much attention to sailboat races. A few races, however, capture the imagination of sailors and landlubbers alike.

The greatest and most historic of these races are the America's Cup Races. They began in 1851, when the New York Yacht Club was invited to compete in the English Yacht Races. Six members of the club built a beautiful 101-foot (30.3-meter) schooner named *America*.

In a single glorious race, the crew of the *America* beat all the English sailors so thoroughly that the British group turned down repeated challenges to compete again. The New York sailors proudly brought home a decorated, massive silver vase called the *Hundred Guineas Cup*. It was later renamed the *America's Cup*.

Ever since that first race, the trophy has been an international challenge cup. This means that a foreign yacht club challenges the boat that represents the New York Yacht Club. The winner of four out of seven races held off of Newport, Rhode Island, takes the America's Cup. The first challenge was made in 1870 by a 198-foot (59.4-meter) British yacht, which lost the race. All 23 challengers since then have also lost, so the New York Yacht Club has had the trophy for over 100 years.

The largest yacht ever to take part in this series of races was the American defender *Reliance*, which sailed in the 1903 competition. Its hull was 144 feet (43.2 meters) long, but the measurement from the tip of the bowsprit to the end of the boom was 201.8 feet (60.54 meters). This huge boat carried a cloud of sail. Such massive vessels finally became too expensive to maintain.

Smaller boats now defend the America's Cup. Today, the boats used as challengers are from a class of sleek and lovely 12-Meters.

Quite different from the America's Cup competition, but just as exciting, is the Single-handed Transatlantic Race. This competition began in 1960 and has since been held every four years. The race is open to any seaworthy boat and to any experienced sailor. The only rule states that the skipper must sail alone. *Wind vane self-steering gears,* a device that frees a sailor from the constant task of steering, made the Single-handed Transatlantic Race possible. This instrument allows a sailor to leave the tiller or wheel and tend the ship, cook meals, and sleep.

The course for the Single-handed Transatlantic Race extends 3,000 miles (4,800 kilometers) from Plymouth, England, to Newport, Rhode Island. Two Frenchmen hold the honor of completing the race faster than anyone else. Alain Colas, on the 70-foot (21-meter) *Pen Duick IV,* and Jean Yves-Terlain, on the mammoth 128-foot (38.4-meter) *Vendredi Treize,* finished the 1972 transatlantic race in 21 days. Some of the slowest competitors have taken as long as 69 days to finish.

A third great race, organized in 1973, went around the world. Four years later, a similar competition took place. Now, the Round-the-World Race is a regular event. The start and finish of this 28,000-mile (44,800-kilometer) competition are at Portsmouth, England. The yachts stop at Capetown, South Africa; Sydney, Australia, or Auckland, New Zealand; and Rio de Janeiro, Brazil. During these three stops, skippers and crew have a chance to repair their gear and rest.

Most of the yachts that take part in this long, difficult race are from 60 to 80 feet (18 to 24 meters) long. Skippers of some of the fastest and most technically advanced boats compete for the prized Round-the-World title.

In this ocean race, the skipper and crew sail around the clock for days. The yachts must carry enough crew members so that half can work on deck while half rest below. Yacht racing on this level costs a lot of money. And in poor weather, a skipper and crew may be damp and cold for several days. Some people say ocean racing is like standing under a cold shower tearing up 100-dollar bills!

Most sailors, however, think that the good times outweigh the bad. Surging along on a sparkling sea is refreshing. And few achievements thrill a sailor more than navigating a perfect course. After days and nights of sailing beyond the sight of land, the boat arrives exactly where it is supposed to. Finishing ahead of the other competitors is even more exciting.

Flyer, a Dutch yacht skippered by Cornelius van Rietschoten, was the winner of the 1980 Whitbread Round-the-World Race.

The tall ships leave the island of Bermuda on June 20, 1976, heading for Newport, Rhode Island. They are on the third and final leg of the bicentennial race, which began in Plymouth, England, on May 2.

Old-time sailing ships compete in San Francisco's Master Mariners Race. The *Klaraborg* (left), built in 1860, is the oldest ship still sailing. The *Arminel*, a 70-foot ketch, was built in 1905.

From time to time, sailors also race the tall ships, those magnificent old square-riggers of bygone days. In 1976, crews raced the world's tall ships to New York to help celebrate the bicentennial anniversary of the United States.

Sailors hold races annually for other grand old ships of the past. San Francisco has its Master Mariners Race. Newport Beach, California, holds a race for *schooners,* two-masted sailboats whose mainmasts are taller than their foremasts. The people of Friendship, Maine, organize races for the lovely old Friendship sloops that originated there.

A young skipper at the helm of a racing sailboat

THE THRILL OF WINNING

Sailboat racing began as the sport of kings. Today, however, almost anyone can enjoy the sport. Sailing clubs are now found throughout the United States. Many encourage the dinghy classes, in which young people are often the skippers. Two national organizations which sponsor local chapters that have special classes for young people are the following:

Boat Owners Associaton of the U.S.
  (BOAT/US)
880 South Pickett Street
Alexandria, VA 22304

U.S. Yacht Racing Union (USYRU)
P.O. Box 209, Goat Island
Newport, RI 02840

Why do so many people love sailboat racing? There is little public glory in the sport. Big crowds seldom come to watch, and the few observers who do attend rarely cheer. In fact, spectators often have a hard time seeing the whole race course. Some find it difficult to determine what the various boats are doing. Nevertheless, few other racing vehicles have captured the hearts and imaginations of their owners the way sailboats have.

The real reward of sailboat racing comes when sailors constantly sharpen their skills in using the natural force of the wind for propulsion. In race after race, sailors tune their boats and equipment, making small improvements each time. If they work hard enough, a skipper and crew may come to know the thrill of winning.

GLOSSARY

bail—To scoop water out of the inside of a boat

beat—To sail into the direction from which the wind is coming; also called *beating to windward* or *on a beat* or *sailing on the wind*

block—A framework containing a pulley that is attached to a boat. A block is used to change the direction of a line or to reduce the amount of strength needed to move a weight.

bowsprit—A piece projecting from the front of a larger sailboat

buoy— A floating object used to mark the perimeter of a channel or other shallow area that a boat should avoid

capsize—To tip over; upset

catspaw—A ripple indicating a bit of wind on an otherwise calm surface of water

celestial navigation—A system that depends on the sun, moon, stars, and planets for keeping a boat on course

channel—A narrow, deep section of water between two shallow areas

cleat—A fitting to which a line can be secured

close to the wind—As near as possible to the direction from which the wind is coming

corrected time—The final time given to each boat in a race. Handicaps are calculated and used to adjust elapsed times to corrected times.

course—The route that a boat is to sail

dinghy—A very small sailboat without a cabin

eddy—A current usually the result of tidal streams as they move around stationary objects. An eddy current runs contrary to the main current in an area.

elapsed time—The time it takes a sailboat to complete the course of a race

genoa—A large *jib*, or sail, set on the front of a boat. It overlaps the mast and stretches far back next to the mainsail.

handicap—A disadvantage given to a boat competing with slower boats from various classes

heel—A boat *heels* when it tips sideways from an upright, vertical position

hike—To sit on the high side of a boat and lean over the water to reduce the degree of heel; also called *hiking out*

line—A rope used on a boat

luff—The leading edge of the sail; also the fluttering of a sail when the boat is sailing too close into the wind, or if the sail is out too far

mark—Any object that indicates part of a race course

one-design class—A racing class in which all boats are built according to the same specifications

plane—To skim across the water, barely touching the surface

playing the main sheet—Controlling a boat by using the main sheet to bring in the mainsail during calm periods and to let it out during gusts of wind

points of sail—The three directions a boat can move in relation to the wind

port tack—A boat sailing with the wind coming over the left side of the boat

protest—An official objection made by a sailor who believes a competitor has broken a racing rule

protest committee—A group of disinterested yacht-club members appointed to listen to both sides of a protest and decide whether a rule was broken

race committee—A group of persons appointed to start a race, observe the participants to be sure no one breaks a rule, and serve as judges at the finish line

reach—To sail with the wind coming across the middle of the side of a boat; also called *reaching* or *on a reach* or *sailing across the wind*

reef—To reduce the area of a sail by partly lowering the sail and tying the bottom portion to the boom; also called *reefing*

reef points—Short pieces of line used to tie down the bottom portion of a sail when it is being reefed

regatta—An event that includes a series of races and festivities held on one day or within a few days of each other

restricted class—A racing class in which boats must meet certain specifications but may also differ from each other in some ways; also called *development class*

right of way—The authority that entitles one boat to hold to its course while others in the area must give way

run—To sail with the wind coming from behind, or over the stern; also called *running* or *on a run* or *sailing before the wind*

schooner—A two-masted sailboat on which the mainmast is taller than the foremast (the mast nearest the bow)

sextant—A navigating instrument that measures vertical and horizontal angles of the sun, moon, and stars

spars—Stout poles that support a boat's arrangement of sails

spinnaker—A large, lightweight sail that may be used when the wind is coming from behind a boat

starboard tack—A boat sailing with the wind coming over the right side of the boat

tack—To take a zigzag course when sailing into the wind; see *beat*

time allowance—A measurement telling how many seconds a boat travels for each mile of a race; used to determine a boat's handicap

trim the sails—To spread the sails to catch the wind after recovering from a capsize

unrestricted class—A racing class in which boats may vary greatly from each other but must also meet some specifications set up by the class association

wind vane self-steering gears—A steering device that guides the boat when a sailor leaves the tiller or wheel

windward—The direction from which the wind is blowing

windward mark—The first turning point in a sailboat race

Airplanes

AEROBATICS
AIRPLANE RACING
HOME-BUILT AIRPLANES
YESTERDAY'S AIRPLANES

Automobiles & Auto Racing

AMERICAN RACE CAR DRIVERS
THE DAYTONA 500
DRAG RACING
ICE RACING
THE INDIANAPOLIS 500
INTERNATIONAL RACE CAR DRIVERS
LAND SPEED RECORD BREAKERS
RALLYING
ROAD RACING
TRACK RACING

CLASSIC SPORTS CARS
DINOSAUR CARS: LATE GREAT CARS
   FROM 1945 TO 1966

KIT CARS: CARS YOU CAN BUILD
   YOURSELF
MODEL CARS
VANS: THE PERSONALITY VEHICLES
YESTERDAY'S CARS

Bicycles

BICYCLE ROAD RACING
BICYCLE TRACK RACING
BICYCLES ON PARADE

Motorcycles

GRAND NATIONAL CHAMPIONSHIP RACES
MOPEDS: THE GO-EVERYWHERE BIKES
MOTOCROSS MOTORCYCLE RACING
MOTORCYCLE RACING
MOTORCYCLES ON THE MOVE
THE WORLD'S BIGGEST MOTORCYCLE RACE:
   THE DAYTONA 200
YESTERDAY'S MOTORCYCLES

Other Specialties

KARTING
SAILBOAT RACING
SKYDIVING
SNOWMOBILE RACING
YESTERDAY'S FIRE ENGINES

Lerner Publications Company
241 First Avenue North, Minneapolis, Minnesota 55401